THE
SKULL
THAT
YAWNS

Anthony Lopez

ISBN 978-1-63784-437-3 (paperback)
ISBN 978-1-63784-438-0 (digital)

Copyright © 2024 by Anthony Lopez

All rights reserved. No part of this publication may be reproduced, distributed, or transmitted in any form or by any means, including photocopying, recording, or other electronic or mechanical methods without the prior written permission of the publisher. For permission requests, solicit the publisher via the address below.

Hawes & Jenkins Publishing
16427 N Scottsdale Road Suite 410
Scottsdale, AZ 85254
www.hawesjenkins.com

Printed in the United States of America

Away he bounds, with little fear and seeks the tangled rough.

—Abraham Lincoln

CONTENTS

Chapter 1: Death Sentence 1
Chapter 2: Southern Strategy 11
Chapter 3: Apache Fire 17
Chapter 4: Lincoln's Nightmare 20
Chapter 5: The Confederate Avenger 22
Chapter 6: Degataga Sends for Goyale 26
Chapter 7: Brother Mangas 28
Chapter 8: Golden Boy Boothe 32
Chapter 9: Doomsday Prepper 38
Chapter 10: The Human Tiger 41

CHAPTER 1

Death Sentence

Lincoln had made a truly harsh decision to execute and make an example out of the Lakota for trespassing. Lincoln was cerebral and accurate in his affairs concerning executions. Honest Abe had enough of these uncivilized filthy heathens. US colonel Henry H. Sibley had reported the murder of five settlers on Dakota territory, or at least "formerly" known as Dakota territory. Lincoln stood up in front of the window at the oval office with his thumbs in his overalls.

Lincoln gazed out of the window at the sun and the beautiful fields of green surrounding the federal White House, and as he was staring at an almond tree dancing in the sunlight through a break in the clouds, a flashback came to Abraham's mind. A different place and a different time, when Lincoln was an eighty-five-pound seven-year-old. Little Abe was out trapping expeditiously with his grandfather and little Abe's uncle Mordecai. Unfortunately for the Lincoln clan that day, they happened to be checking traps sixteen miles northeast of their family owned settlement that happened to be Sauk Indian territory. This was a defining moment for the young Abraham Lincoln. For after this day, he would never be the same.

As they were fixing an empty trap, three arrows hit his grandfather right in his chest, and as he fell backward from the force, Little Abraham immediately jumped to his grandfather's side and could see blood gurgling from his grandpa's mouth.

"Run, Abraham, run," his grandpa said one last time.

Little Abraham grabbed his grandfather's hand and, with tears in his eyes, cried, "No, Grandpa, no!"

Simultaneously, arrows flew by as Mordecai reached for his colt, fully loaded, to chase away the ambush. Abraham's grandpa left his body before his eyes, and as he went to hug his grandfather for the last time, a Sauk warrior on horseback snatched him up, his hand like an eagle claw. Thankfully, Uncle Mordecai timely reached his pistol while avoiding incoming fire and shot the horseback warrior in the back of his head through the holster, causing him to drop Abraham.

Uncle Mordecai and the Sauk Indians had a shootout, but Mordecai had the better aim. The last two warriors ran off to fight another day.

Little Abraham was crying and reaching for his grandfather as his uncle picked him up and shouldered him in a full sprint the whole way back to the estate. The horrific memory was tattooed into the president's mind.

A flock of geese flew over the White House squawking, and Abraham came to his senses.

"There is no room for ruthless savagery in our new civilized world! All must be civil, kind, and in a delighted spirit," Lincoln said out loud. "I will make an example of those uncivilized heathens! It will be a spectacle of punishable death! Solidifying savagery will not be tolerated," he finished.

Honest Abe was blessed by God to bring justice and stability to the newfound world. It was a chosen responsibility Lincoln took very seriously. The issue was, the indigenous natives would not bow down. They would not work, and they would not accept their newly appointed territories. Nor would they accept Jesus Christ in the name of civilization. Why were these heathens so far behind in technology? The heathens did not obey rules, and it was the federal union's self-righteous duty to civilize the entire western frontier. And that was why God brought the White European man to this newfound land to save the souls of these mountain witches and savages.

Ole' Abraham Lincoln felt no mercy and no remorse. His terrible childhood memories of his grandfather's brutal murder by savages haunted him in the back of his mind. It had been decades since his papa was senselessly arrowed down like an animal of game.

Honest Abe had the memory of an elephant. He remembered the incident like it was yesterday. Abraham told Father Thomas reminds of the story so many times to remind him of how far Lincoln had traveled to this point.

Our sixteenth president was named after Capitan Abe, and they were very close. "Papa" taught young Abraham to fish, trap, build, and be a strong leader. The ambush left a bloody stain on the Lincoln family tree, the same infamous conspiracy of which grandson Abraham "the Honest" would similarly succumb.

Ole Honest Abe would finally have a chance at revenge and redemption in the largest mass execution in American history. Honest Abe would make an example of unruly native factions across the newfound land. Papa would be proud. Four hundred and seventy-five natives would be charged with trespassing and murder. Forty of these long-haired bastard redskins were to be sentenced to death by hanging. President number 16 would make a massive statement! Not only was he going to hang them, but he would also humiliate them by building a grand stage theater of death. Lincoln's executive order was to construct a large stage that would measure a hundred feet in square diameter, and he ordered all convicted to be hung simultaneously to show of force that savagery would not be tolerated. This would prove the White man's technology would ultimately be the engineered genocide of their very species if the indigenous refused to obey the program.

More than half of Lincoln's advisory administration staff voted strongly against the mass execution. However, between his deep-seated hatred for the red man and for the sake of a civilized future union, Lincoln proceeded to have a scribe write up a conviction letter and death sentence contract for the forty Lakota Indians, to be put to death before the outbreak of war and also for raiding innocent wagon camps and accusing them of rape. Lincoln was pulling out all the stops on this crusade.

Therefore, Abraham Lincoln, the sixteenth president of the United States, wrote a letter of justification to the federal judiciary congress for mass execution:

> Anxious to not act with so much clemency as to encourage another outbreak of war on one hand, nor with so much severity as to be cruel to one another. I ordered a careful examination of the records of the trials to be made against the Lakota Indians. In view I first order the execution of such miscreants proved guilty of murder, theft, and the violation of females. And lastly, I have written down the names of thirty-nine individuals whom participated in this melee that lead to the death of seven innocent civilians, of this incident all thirty-nine of the names on this list are sentence to death by hanging by executive order of the federal union.
>
> Signed,
>
> Abraham Lincoln

Originally, Lincoln ordered forty Lakota to death. However, one of the forty Lakota was dying of sickness. And the day before the execution, one Lakota committed suicide by chain choke.

Guilty Parties

1. Tipi-Hdo-Niche
2. Wyata-Tonwan
3. Taju-Xa
4. Hinhan-Shoun-Koyag-Mani
5. Maza-Bomidu
6. Wapa-Duta
7. Wahena

8. Sna-Mani
9. Radapinyanke
10. Dowanniye
11. Xunkaska
12. Hepan
13. Tunkan-Ichi-Tamani
14. Ite-Duta
15. Amdacha
16. Hepidan
17. Marpiya Te Najin
18. Henry Millord
19. Chaska Dan Little
20. Baptiste Campbell
21. Tate Kage
22. Hapinkpa
23. Hypolite Auge
24. Nape Shuha
25. Wakan Tanka
26. Tunkan Koyag Inajin
27. Maka Te Najin
28. Paza Kuta Mani
29. Tate Hoo Dan
30. Waxican Na
31. Aichaga
32. Ho Tan Inku
33. Ce Tan Hunka
34. Hadhin Hda
35. Chanka Hdo
36. Oyate Tonwan
37. Mehu We Mea
38. Wakinyan Na
39. Wakanozan
40. Shako Pee

Like father like nation, Lincoln's hatred for the red man was so obvious, and his disdain for the indigenous race trickled down the federal totem pole. For all who served Lincoln felt this animosity and absorbed it was well. For as leaders as followers, these union birds of a feather flocked together.

And in reality, the natives were relentlessly attacking, ambushing, and assaulting the pioneer wagon caravans of the newly entering and invading White settlers from all over the world. Now the federal union would use native trackers to catch natives. However, federal scout or not, the federal vision heathens were not to be trusted, so as soon as a federally employed savage tracked down the savage wanted at that moment, the scouts would be jailed with the general population of prisoners of war, regardless of their accomplishments while on duty. It was early December 1862 when the Honest One decided to hang the Lakota in front of the world. Lincoln was smack-dab in the middle of the war, and he knew he would have to be drastic in his execution.

Between the Lakota wars theater and Comanche war theater and the Apache war campaign, Lincoln was feeling overwhelmed, and these emotions led to his decision of a public execution to make a point. Now the federal union was losing ground on several fronts of the war. The Lincoln administration would bring a lot of overpowering force to the Indians and to the confederacy, for not only would they break the spirit of the natives (the Federal Union would declare the Emancipation Proclamation to free the 3.1 million slaves helping the confederacy to farm their agriculture) but also the slaves' contributions to the Confederacy Army.

The Lincoln administration would deliver a one-two punch to push forward and win the war once and for all.

Lincoln was thinking to himself. Honest Abe had been preparing the African American audience to his sympathies of the culture and the future of their race. In fact, it had only been four and a half months since Abraham performed a speech in Washington, DC, in front of a mixed audience of both African and newly arrived Europeans. Lincoln was now having flashbacks of this speech.

THE SKULL THAT YAWNS

August 14, 1862

Your race is suffering, in my judgment, the greatest wrong inflicted on any people. But even when you cease to be slaves, you are yet far removed from being placed on an equality with the white race. You are cut off from many of the advantages which the other race enjoys. The aspiration of men is to enjoy equality with the best when free but on this broad continent, not a single man of your race is made equal to a single man of ours. Go where you are treated the best, and the ban is still upon you. I do not propose to discuss this but to present it as a fact with which we have to deal with these unpleasantries. I cannot alter it, if I could I would. It is a fact about which we all think and feel alike, I and you. We look to our condition. Owing to the existence of the two races on this continent, I need not recount to you the effects upon white men, growing out of the institution of slavery.

I believe in its general evil effects on the white race. See our present condition, the country engaged in war; our white men cutting one another's throats, none knowing how far it will extend and then consider what we know to be the truth. But for your race among us there could not be war, although many men engaged on either side do not care for you one way or the other.

Nevertheless, I repeat, without the institution of slavery and colored race as basis. The war could not have existed. It is better for us both, therefore, to be separated.

I know that there are free men among you, even if they could better their condition, are not as much inclined to go out of the country as those who, being slaves, could obtain their freedom on this condition. I suppose one of the principal difficulties in the way of colonization is that free colored man cannot see that his comfort would be advanced by it.

You may believe that you can live in Washington, or elsewhere, in the United States the remainder of your life as easily. Perhaps more so, than you can in any foreign country; and hence you may come to the conclusion that you have nothing to do with the idea of going to a foreign country.

This is, and I speak and no unkind sense, an extremely selfish view of the case. You ought to do something to help those who are not so fortunate as yourself. There is an unwillingness on the part of our people, harsh as it may be, for you free colored people to remain with us.

Now, if you could give a start to the White people, you would open a wide door for many to be made free. If we deal with those who are not free at the beginning, and who's intellects are clouded by slavery, we have very poor material to start with. if intelligent colored men, such as before me now [the likes of Frederick Douglas and Harriet Tubman were present]. Would move in this manner, much might be accomplished.

It is exceedingly important that we have men at the beginning capable of thinking as white men, and not those who have been systematically oppressed. There is much to encourage you for the sake of your race. You should sacrifice something of your present comfort for the purpose of being as grand in that respect as the white people. It is a cheering thought throughout life, that something can be done to ameliorate the condition of those who have been subject to the hard usages of the world.

It is difficult to make a man miserable while he feels he is worthy of himself and claims kinder to the great God who made him, so with that being said;

The colony of Liberia has been in existence a very long time. In a certain sense it is a success... The question is, if the colored people are persuaded to go anywhere. Well why not "Liberia." One reason for unwillingness to do so is that some of you would rather remain within reach of the country of your nativity.

I do not know how much attachment you may have toward a race. It does not strike me that you have the greatest reason to love them. But yet you are attached to them, at all events. The place I am thinking about for a colony is in Central America; the country is a very excellent one for any people and with great natural resources and advantages, and especially because of the similarity of climate with your native soil, thus being suited to your physical condition.

The particular place I have in view is to be a great highway from the Atlantic or Caribbean Sea to the Pacific Ocean, and this particular place has all the advantages for a colony. The practical thing I want to ascertain is, whether I can get a number of able-bodied men, with their wives and children, who are willing to go when I present evidence of encouragement and protection. Could I get a hundred tolerably intelligent men, with their wives and children and able to "cut their own fodder" so to speak. Can I have fifty? if I could find twenty-five able-bodied men, with a mixture of women and children, good things in the family relation.

I think I can make it a successful commencement. I want you to let me know whether this can be done or not. This is the Practical part of my wish to see you. These are subjects of a very great importance, worthy of the month study, instead of a speech delivered in an hour.

I asked you, then to consider seriously, not pertaining to yourselves merely, nor for your race and ours for the present time, but as one of the things, if successfully managed, for the good of mankind, not confined to the present generation but as… [Lincoln cleared his throat for the speech's grand finale]

From age to age descends the lay to millions yet to be, till far it echoes roll away into eternity.

As Lincoln looked around, he noticed that a lot of his audience were shaking their heads in disbelief. Harriet Tubman leaned over to whisper in Frederick Douglass's ear, "So you mean to tell me Masta Lincoln gone free us to win his war then ship us off to South America? What the hell? What if we board the ship and they sink it?"

It was a serious dilemma for the soon-to-be free men. The slaves did not know who to trust at this point in this speech. Lincoln was saying three different things. First, he said "I will free you once you fight in the Union army." Two is to "fight in my Army." And three, "Once we win the war, I plan on sending all colored people to Liberia or South America to colonize."

Not only was Lincoln doing speeches professing the colonization of the slaves, he was also freeing the slaves to finish the war and save the Union as precious and perfect as it was. Now that Lincoln had completed the speech, his plan to exterminate the Indians and free the slaves was en route for success. And once these tasks were completed, Lincoln would finally slaughter the South into submission and win the war and the new world.

CHAPTER 2

Southern Strategy

Richmond, Virginia

Meanwhile, at the Jefferson Davis executive mansion, the Confederate elite men, generals, female spies. and governors elite war council meeting concerning the newfound letter exposing Lincoln's future plans. The letter was stolen from Horace Greeley, who was a publisher and a writer for the *New York Tribune*. Rose O'Neal Greenhow was a socialite and a friend of Mr. Greeley. Also, she was a Confederate spy.

Rose Greenhow was at the top of her class in a Confederate pool of female spies. The only other Confederate female spy who was as cunning if not more than Greenhow was Bell Boyd. Rose Greenhow had a high status in the previous Buchanan administration and had a lot of trust among the modern society. All in attendance were gathered around a large wooden table with a Masonic emblem all over. Rose stood up and unraveled the letter. As she opened the letter, she began to read aloud. All eyes were on her. She cleared her throat and looked around the room with intense eyes.

"Lincoln wrote, 'Dear sir, I have just read yours of the nineteenth addresses to myself through the *New York Tribune*. If there be in it any statements of assumptions of fact which I may know erroneous, I do not know and here, convert them. If there be in it any inferences which I may believe to be falsely drawn, I do not, now in here, argue against them. If there be perceptible in it and impatient and dictatorial tone, I wave it in deference to an old friend whose heart I have always supposed to be right. As to the policy I seem to be pursuing, as you say, I have not meant to leave anyone in doubt. I would save the union. I would save it in the shortest way under the constitution. The sooner the National Authority can be restored, the near the union will be the Union as it was.

"'If there be those who would not save the union unless they could at the same time destroy slavery, I do not agree with them! My paramount objective in this struggle is to save the union, and is not either to save or to destroy slavery. If I could save the union without freeing any slave, I would do it, and if I could save the Union by freeing all the slaves, I would do it. And if I could save the Union by freeing some slaves and leaving others alone, I would also do that. What I do about slavery and the colored race, I do because I believe it helps to save the union, and what I forbear because I do not believe it would help me to save the union. I shall do less whenever I shall believe what I am doing hurts the cause, And I shall do more whenever I shall believe doing more will help the cause.

"'I shall try to correct errors when shown to be errors, and I shall adopt new views so fast as they shall appear to be true views. I have stated my purpose according to my view of official duty, and I intend no modification of my oft-expressed personal wish that all men everywhere could be free'" (signed, Abraham Lincoln).

Rose Greenhow cleared her throat and handed the letter to Robert E. Lee, who was sitting at the table. This letter was passed around at this Confederate council meeting. This letter would be used against Lincoln to convince the current slaves that they were being set up for failure. Many strategies would be discussed at this meeting. All in attendance were concerned on how the situation was going.

The president of the Confederacy, Jefferson Davis, was at the head of the table as he spoke.

"Our new government is founded upon exactly the opposite ideas. It's foundations are laid down before us, and its cornerstone rest upon it, that the obvious great truth that the Negro is not at all equal to the White man. That slavery, subordination to the superior race, in his natural and moral condition. This idea is our newfound government, is the first, in the history of the world, in human history as we know it, based upon this great physical, philosophical, and moral truth!"

Everyone in attendance nodded their approval. Vice President of the Confederacy Alexander H. Stephens continued the speech as if practice.

"Our slaves are critical to our war machine. Every Black slave wielding a shovel releases a White man for our ranks." Stephens slapped both of his hands on the Masonic table before his empty chair. "They are loading and transporting and unloading supplies! The slaves are digging trenches and building roads, erecting barricades. They are constructing fortifications, preparing and building railroads. and they are building bridges, trestles, and tunnels! And let's not forget our slaves' most precious and time-consuming tasks. Most importantly, they are cooking food for the massive army of men, and they run the kitchen so our White soldiers can eat and focus on battle and not cook and wonder what to eat for morale's sake. Our slaves are tailoring the soldiers' uniforms. Also, we cannot afford to lose such a great asset as our Black workforce, for they're vital to win this war! That damn Yankee is going to try and set them free and planting seeds of thought so they can equalize the White man! The slaves in Texas have already abandoned post! We need to tell our slaves it's a trap and that they are being set up for failure!"

Stephens was passionate in his words as if the world was crumbling before him.

Stephens continued as he looked around at the table of elites. "And in Louisiana, they started the colored Louisiana Native Guard and the Kansas Colored Guard. And in my opinion, the worst by far, First South Carolina colored volunteers, who hired their slave masters to fight alongside the slaves! And by far the worst reported incident is that damn deserter Robert Smalls, stealing a Confederate warship, the *Planter*." Stephens gasped, both exasperated and exhausted by his speech. "We must absolutely and resolutely assassinate Ole Honest Abe Lincoln. Now he threatened us and our succession to return to the union by January 1 of the year of our dear Lord 1863. It's been weeks past that deadline. Ole Honest Abe is doing everything he can to coerce our Negro soldiers to abandon their posts and escape their masters, and it's working. Therefore, I propose sending our best men after Lincoln. We will send Mosby and his Rangers. Or better yet, we can send John Jackson Dickison to raid and ambush that bastard."

Stephens chuckled as he looked to his left, searching new ideas. He suddenly studied the red man at the table in a difference of opinion. Stephens thought out loud, "And even maybe send General Watie's first mounted rifles and horseman? Do any of you gentlemen have any good ideas? And remember, before you answer, Honest Abe is the most guarded man in the world with his newfound 'men of Secret Service in black uniforms.' Ha! What a joker. This new battalion is specifically guarding him and his family."

Everyone in the war room looked around at one another, puzzled by such a critical question. No one in the war council really wanted to speak up with the wrong answer. Also present at the Confederate war council meeting were a few native Confederate generals, Major Broken Arm of the Osage Cavalry Battalion and Brigadier General Stand Watie of the First Cherokee Mounted Rifles. They looked right at each other as if they were both thinking the same thing, which they were.

After a slight delay, General Watie replied, "I know of a soul who can penetrate the union security and officially assassinate Lincoln!"

Attendee Braxton Bragg, who was a general, also replied to his former West Point colleague, "Who? You think we should send the Bushwhackers or Frank and Jesse James? Mosby or Dickison? Who?"

"Well," said General Watie. "Due to the fact we are all currently on our missions and campaigns at hand, I believe what we need to do is hire a faction of individuals who are unattached to our cause yet someone who equally hates Tall Hat just as much as we do and who has a grievance toward the Union—"

But before General Watie could finish his sentence, General Albert Gallatin Jenkins rudely interrupted his red counterpart and said, "Now just wait a minute, General Watie. However, we gave a plethora of inside sources to remedy this Lincoln issue. I say we to send Bloody Bill!"

General Officer Stonewall Jackson replied, for Jackson was passionate on Caucasian stoicism. The Big Cheese himself, Jefferson Davis, was a calm and calculated character.

"General Jackson," President Davis said sternly. "Brigadier General Stand Watie has major experiences in his campaign and is also educated properly. After all, we already sent Maria Bell Boyd to stay and infiltrate the North territory, along with her intel. And after several assassination attempts by some of our top soldiers and West Point graduates like Frisby McCullough and the Border Ruffians, the waters are extremely rough. We have to close our colleges and redirect the professors and students' cause, and there are few masters on their plantations to thicken their ranks. We are shorthanded as it is, so I believe if we can outsource this assassination with a guarantee, it would be a most wise choice to keep everyone in the post that they are currently at. At this moment in time, it would not be smart to shuffle the ranks, so, General Watie, whoever you have in mind, do you guarantee his work?"

General Watie nodded with a smirk. "It is not guaranteed. It is a promise!"

Vice President Alexander H. Stephens had to put his two cents in on the matter. "Whoa, whoa, wait a minute now, General Watie. I hope you're not implying hiring anyone from your race, because there will be no red man heroes in this war! So I must know of whom you're implying on reaching out to concerning this matter."

General Stand rebutted, "Goyale is what my people call him. However, your people know him as Geronimo the Apache, a known horse thief who has been on a murder rampage since 1851. He is on fire for Tall Hat's death for the Mankota massacre, and he and his people are not like me and my people. He is uneducated and a rogue. Only good at killing men and stealing horses!"

General Watie defended his choice. Stonewall Jackson looked at both his men. "Now, gentlemen, I have shown favoritism to my friends and family thus far, so I believe it is wise to outsource also!"

Then Vice President Stephens said, "Okay, fine. But no red men heroes, so we will also outsource a cover-up White man hero. A Confederate avenger poster boy, so to speak. To help boost morale among our soldiers. A successful White man that they can all look up to and hang onto their hope that we will win this war and save our way of living. Amen."

CHAPTER 3

Apache Fire

It was a dark starry night in the New Mexico desert. Geronimo was praying to the skies with tears in his eyes. The crisp spring evening breeze was blowing his shoulder-length and battled-hardened hair, and a sudden wind blew the fire's smoke away from his direction, as if to avoid him. Geronimo was arguing with the clouds in the sky. He was brokenheartedly screaming his case to a wail and back and suddenly dancing.

The horseback desert warriors were so shocked to see their mostly quiet chief warrior's outburst with such emotion he never displayed. Not one warrior had witnessed a reckless display of emotions since Geronimo's family, including his mom, his wife, and two daughters, were senselessly murdered by a band of raiding Mexican soldiers, two decades before the outbreak of the war.

Young Geronimo was on a hunting quest to gather meat for winter season on that tragic day just to return to his burnt and raided village. This caused him to eventually race off to the mountains and climb the tallest mountain he could find to pray to his higher power, Ussen. He stayed on that mountain and fasted. The sky opened and blessed Geronimo with fortitude and immortality. Geronimo had been a shaman ever since.

Earlier that day, in January 1863, a Lakota chief and messenger hand delivered a New York printed newspaper, *Pioneer Press*, and on the front cover was a graphic illustration of thirty-eight Dakota brothers being executed by hanging off a massive constructed death table. Many artists and illustrators were present at the country's biggest group of execution in recorded history because of President Lincoln enforcing a no flash photo public policy. There were over ten thousand people in attendance for this death concert that "Tall Hat" orchestrated.

Geronimo gazed at the newspaper photo with tears in his eyes. The Apache chief was devastated at the despicable display of inhumanity. This illustrative image struck a black chord in Geronimo's heart. The Apache chief could not help but feel a bit guilty, and only because two years before in 1861, the Lakota grand war council had summoned Geronimo to a war meeting. However, between the Mexicans and the European invaders fighting among each other, the Apache chief had way too much on his plate, so he could not travel and attend at that time.

The Grand Lakota war council included Sitting Bull, Crazy Horse, Red Leaf, Two Moons, Chief Gall, Buffalo Calf Road Woman, and many, many others. There were tribal leaders from 60 percent of all First Nations. The Lakota were an advanced tribe. They shared gunsmith technology and geographical survival techniques with the British since the 1600s. The Lakota were attempting to form a First Nations unit. However, it was too late for all that. Besides, European invasion was in full swing, and so was the struggle to be the king of America.

Abraham and Jefferson were in all-out war. The indigenous people also understood the world of red, yellow, Black, and White races would never be the same. The old world was on its deathbed, and a new country would emerge. The winner would take all. Geronimo knew it was the final countdown, and he would have to focus all his energy on exacting his revenge. Geronimo also knew that he could not accomplish his goal alone. He would have to form a trustworthy team, and they were going to need training and experience to the Apache chief's specifications. He knew he would have to handpick a group of elite warriors and train them for the main event.

THE SKULL THAT YAWNS

Chief Geronimo had suffered a pinch of guilt for not previously joining the First Nations Confederacy. Maybe he could have prevented Tall Hat's scheme of death. Maybe not.

Geronimo looked up at Red Leaf on his horse and said, "Where do I find this monster who is responsible for this flex?"

He gathered himself from his emotional breakdown.

"It is Tall Hat," replied Red Leaf. "He lives in DC, and he is the most protected man in the world."

You see, Lincoln had declared war on the Lakota and the Apache in the summer of 1862. This was the last straw for Geronimo. All the First Nations warriors had heard of the ultimate warrior Geronimo. This was it. He was chosen, and he was obligated to plot the murder of Tall Hat at all costs, including death. For it would be the Apache chief's greatest chapter in his life quest. Eye for an eye, tooth for a tooth. Chief Geronimo was disgusted and brokenhearted for his thirty-eight brothers of the north, and he vowed to stop Tall Hat and anybody who stepped in his way.

CHAPTER 4

Lincoln's Nightmare

Meanwhile, in the Union White House, President Lincoln was in his Oval Office and reeling in his mind over the newly thwarted ambush in the Battle of Antietam. Lincoln would pull his cabinet together again for a war meeting concerning the Emancipation Proclamation. Lincoln's new election was causing severe drama for himself and his legion. Lincoln was receiving at least twenty death threats a day. Therefore, Lincoln initiated a group of West Point graduates as his and his family's personal safety guards. He appointed Ambrose Burnside as captain of men of the Secret Service.

After pacing the office, Lincoln grew sleepy and lay down on the office couch and fell fast asleep. Lincoln began dreaming again. He was back on his family farm wearing his grandpa's captain hat.

His grandpa said, "Remember, Abraham, a man is remembered for his hat, not his hair." And he belly laughed as an arrow flew into his chest.

Lincoln was crying and tossing and turning in his sleep.

"Wake up, Abraham. Wake up," repeated Mary Todd as she shook her husband.

Lincoln sat up in a cold sweat as he awoke.

"Are you okay, sweetheart?" The concerned wife handed her husband a glass of water. "I almost put the glass of water on you to wake you, Abraham!"

Abraham replied, "I'm okay, dear. I just have a lot on my mind."

Lincoln summoned his new security guard captain, Ambrose Burnside, into his office.

"Yes, Commander. How can I be of service?" asked Captain Burnside.

"Have Kit Carson round up the Apache, the Lakota, and the Winnebagos. I want them all on appointed Indian reservations yesterday. And if they resist, shoot them on sight! I have had enough of the red man race, and my goal is to blot them off the map for eternity!" said Lincoln.

Mary Todd and Captain Burnside were shocked by Abraham's emotional orders, for the president was cool, calm, and collected 99 percent of the time.

"Sir, yes, sir," Ambrose replied. "I will contact Kit Carson immediately, and we shall round up all those savages and force their civility, or else it's death for them!"

"You're dismissed, Ambrose," said Lincoln, still emotionally disturbed from his nightmare.

Captain Burnside silently nodded his head as he exited and closed the door behind him.

Mary Todd hugged her husband back and looked him in the eyes. "I love you, Abraham, and I will pray for you," his wife reassured him. "Now let me go back to the kitchen to finish our tea cake for dinner, honey."

"I love you too, dear." He kissed Mary Todd on the forehead just before she could rise up off the couch and head toward the kitchen.

CHAPTER 5

The Confederate Avenger

Back in Richmond, Virginia, at the Confederacy capitol, was yet another emergency war meeting for the Southern states. In the Scottish Reich war room, all present, including President Davis, were growing desperate in his defense systems in the war. President Davis ironically was a former member of the Democratic Party for the Union state of Mississippi. Also, the president of the Confederacy was the former secretary of war and served from 1853 to 1857 under President Franklin Pierce.

Also present at the emergency meeting were General Lee, Vice President Alexander H. Stephens, and several generals including Jubal Anderson Early and General Ambrose Powell Hill. And among the war council of Confederates, probably the most important was general idealist Cherokee Stand Watie.

"Greetings, everyone," said President Davis. "It is a very critical time, and we have intel from all across the board. Our credible source, Bell Boyd, has new information regarding the Union's plan to destroy key bridges around Port Royal. However, I have been working closely with General Stonewall to intercept warships and strategic placement of heavy artillery."

President Davis continued, "Strategy is vital to our success in this war, and I want to personally thank Ms. Bell Boyd for her services to her country. Ms. Boyd, stand up!"

THE SKULL THAT YAWNS

The president started to clap as Bell Boyd stood up out of her chair and grabbed her dress sides and a made a proper bow.

"Okay, now have a seat, Ms. Boyd," the president said, nodding and smiling. He continued, "We have land war in Tennessee, the Maryland land war, and the North Carolina land war in the east. Between this chaos and the Battle of Antietam and this confusing Emancipation Proclamation, we must take extreme measures. Now, Captain John Mosby and his posse did a wonderful job capturing Union General Edwin Stoughton, and it was General Stoughton's division that revealed that ole Abraham likes the theater shows and that he has been frequently attending the Ford Theater in Washington, DC. I mean, with all these land wars and naval wars and with all the deserters, I figure we ought to just nip this situation in the bud. Now we have attempted twice to assassinate Lincoln, but his army of secret men are impenetrable. Now John Mosby couldn't pull it off in civil clothing. We have also lost Major General John Stevens Bowen, who was sent for the first assassination attempt. Therefore, I have thought about this many nights in war on the battlefield or in the war council. Abraham is on his toes, so we must get him while he is relaxed and entertained. Now should we go with this General Watie's idea from last meeting?"

Vice President Stephens added his voice. "Well, I do believe this plan to be bulletproof. As of right now, our worst nightmare is coming to fruition. The northern industrial complex is sprawling our way. This industrial war machine will spill blood and oil all over our Southern plantations. The Union is now attempting to build railroads all over the South using the Chinese to spread their iron will to destroy our country. Those damn Yankees have threatened to confiscate and to seize our assets, and one of the main assets they want is our land and gold, on the premise that a slave-owning country is no longer viable. Now we all went to West Point and have all received the same military training and tactical education training. A lot of us served alongside in the Mexican War in 1846. Therefore, we must think outside the box of standard military techniques at such a critical and possible victory in this war. We must take out this king, and his kingdom will fall as well!" exclaimed Stephens.

Stephens pointed to Watie. "Okay, General Stand, who do you have in mind?" Stephens asked with a poker face.

General Watie of the First Mounted Cherokee Braves stood up as he cleared his throat. *Here goes nothing*, Watie thought to himself before he spoke. "President Davis, Vice President Stephens, I know a red brother who can accomplish the goal you have in mind."

All eyes were on him because of his credentials, including West Point graduate and now principal chief of the Cherokee nation. And he had allegiance to the Confederacy battles, including the Battle of Wilson's Creek, Battle of Pea Ridge, and the most recent Battle of Prairie Grove, where he was stationed for the trans-Mississippi campaign. Plus, he was in the Georgia militia at the war's beginning.

"In my realm." Stand paused as he looked around the Southern war council. "In my realm, there is an abundance of information. We all have heard of Geronimo the Apache. When he found out by messenger about Tall Hat hanging thirty-eight Lakota brothers, he swore vengeance against Tall Hat."

"Woah. Now wait a minute," Stephens rudely interrupted. "No red man heroes, General."

Watie questioned, "What do you mean no red man heroes?"

Stephens answered the general, "Exactly what I mean. No red man is going to take all the credit for the assassination of the most public figure in modern history. Hell now, I won't allow it! Besides, we don't know who this Apache has allegiance too."

Stand rebutted, "Geronimo the Apache is his own entity. He swears allegiance only to his God Ussen and his band of Chiricahua Apache!"

General Stonewall Jackson, who was in favor of this idea, jumped in and said, "It is most true about Geronimo the Apache. His allegiance is to his tribe only. I met ole Geronimo before the secession. He hates Mexicans more than any other race of people because the Mexicans are responsible for the deaths of his mother, wife, and children. He told me this when we crossed paths in Lubbock, Texas, at a special meeting between the Comanche and the Texas militia. Geronimo was there for information on a wanted fugitive who raided his camp and stole his favorite pistol."

Stephens was not convinced, but he was desperate. To outsource or not to outsource, that was the question in his head as he looked at the ceiling and began to twiddle his thumbs.

General Watie was sure of this idea, and General Stonewall backed him. Stand had one last thing to say. "Vice President, I know this man is on a whole other level of hate. If anyone can get past Tall' Hat's security detail, I know Geronimo the Apache can. I know if we explain that he will not get credit for the assassination, I'm sure he won't mind. All he wants is Tall Hat's precise location at the precise time."

So Stephens agreed and said, "Okay. We will do the outsource, but we will do it my way, and what I mean by my way is we will have ole Geronimo as a guest assassin. However, we will hire a white man hero who will take all the credit for this. A Confederate avenger so to speak, we need to boost the morale of our Southern soldiers. And I have the perfect character and plot in mind." Stephens took a pause to grin.

"Well, what did you have in mind?" asked Davis.

"This is my plan," said Stephens. "This must be a stealth mission. No guns, no booms, so we can have ole Geronimo stab Lincoln, and our very own Confederate avenger will *boom* shoot that damn tyrant in the face!"

"Okay, I see," said Davis. "Who do you have in mind?"

Stephens replied," Someone we all know and love. And the best part yet, someone on the inside. Actor John Wilkes Booth! He will get all the credit!"

"Quick question," asked Stonewall Jackson. "How do you know that John is on board with your idea?"

Stephens would answer Mr. Stonewall, "Gold, my friend. Gold can buy any soul."

The vice president smiled.

CHAPTER 6

Degataga Sends for Goyale

General Stand Watie sent Geronimo a messenger to meet in a secret location in Oklahoma. Geronimo believed the message, but he was reluctant. Still, he was willing to work with others to get his hands on Tall Hat. Now the Apache and the Cherokee didn't care for each other. Still, they met up face-to-face.

At the Oklahoma location, upon arrival, each chief had twenty warriors with them. All were on horseback. The location was in Laughton and was untouched by White settlers, for this was designated Indian territory by both the warring governments. Both warriors were fierce on either side. Now their chiefs appeared similar in appearance with shoulder-length mourning hair, but other than that, the Apache and the Cherokee were a different savage. The Cherokee had been in contact with the White settlers a lot sooner than the Apache. Therefore, the Cherokee tribe technologies and education were superior to that of the Apache desert folk. The Cherokee were also a taller bunch being they were from flatter lands. The exception was Mangas Coloradas, a unique larger-than-life Apache at six foot and six inches. However, the majority of Apache were short and stocky. Shorter legs made it easier to climb mountains.

Geronimo and Stand met in the middle of the circle that kind of automatically formed as both chiefs gathered. They shook arms, and the general felt uncomfortable, but General Stand, AKA the Degataga, began to speak.

"Well, Goyale, the graycoat white eyes want to work with you in collaboration to kill Tall Hat. But there is no reward, and you must kill him as quietly as possible, for you will not get credit publicly or at all for that matter."

Geronimo thought to himself about how none of that mattered to him at all. All he wanted was a personal meeting with Tall Hat to knock him down a few pegs. So Geronimo looked at the red general in a gray coat and nodded.

"All I want is a handpicked team. I will train them for a while at this handpicked location. And I will take care of everything else!" Geronimo explained.

"Okay," replied General Watie. "Is there anything else you will need?"

"Well," Geronimo thought. "My location will be in the Colorado mountains. I will need weapons, artillery, and food rations."

The general interrupted, "But, Geronimo, no noise in this assassination. Rifles outside only. No noise inside the building!"

"Trust me, Degataga. I got this. Consider Tall Hat dead!"

Deep down, Brigadier General Stand Watie knew this was a promise, not a threat.

"Okay, Geronimo. I will keep in contact. Let me know when you have your team assembled and ready for training. And then I will have Red Leaf bring your rations and ammunition if it is approved by President Davis."

Geronimo nodded in approval as he rode off in the mist with his band of warriors following him.

CHAPTER 7

Brother Mangas

Deep in the heart of the New Mexico desert, between Vegas and Concha Lake, a meeting of Apache nation, all the chiefs and war leaders, were present. A roll call of Nana, Lolo, Vitorio, Cochise, Apache Kid, Chief Black Knife, Lozen, Dahteste, and many others. Geronimo had sent a messenger to the north to summon his brothers of the northern direction. Also present from other tribes were Chief Smoke, Crazy Horse, Rain in the Face, Red Cloud, and Red Leaf the messenger, Kiowa leader Satanta, and the only female present from the north territories, Buffalo Calf Road Woman. Others were present from the south or below Apache Pass. The Civil War had not yet reached the southeast Dragoon Mountains, and the heavily bushed foothills proved to be a safe location to hold one of Turtle Island's most notorious preemptive strike native war council.

 The brothers from the north traveled far to reach this destination. However, the indigenous people traveled trails thousands of miles in length to reach every corner of Turtle Island for thousands of years. There was a makeshift campfire, and everyone sat around with their blankets covering them. It was a solemn moment with all the genocide and war going on in their lives and all around them.

 "I can no longer contain my words," started Mangas Coloradas, Apache. "I must speak." So he stood up, six foot six tall, unusual for a mountain native. Only Lakota Chief Smoke matched his height. "I have been offered a peace treaty by Union general JR West. He has promised food and shelter for the Apache. I trust him, and I can't do this anymore."

His chief interrupted, "Brother, I would advise you not to trust the white eye. Look what they did to compa."

Lozen, an Apache medicine woman who was Vitorio's little sister and entrusted medicine woman, agreed with Geronimo. "Brother, you need not go! I had a vision that you were bitten by a white snake, and his venom killed you. Brother, don't go."

Vitorio agreed. "Brother, I know you are tired. But war is all around, and even the white eyes murdered their brothers. Bluecoats against graycoats, white eyes they have.

"My brother, you are red man. The Whites have no mercy on you. After all, Tall Hat just murdered thirty-eight of our northern brothers mercilessly, and you trust the bluecoat government. You are blinded by your hunger, brother. Besides, we are here to discuss our plan to collaborate with the graycoats, and we need your assistance. I know you're shook from the Apache Pass incident. But it's all-out war right now, and my advice to you is to not trust General West. He is a snake, like his commander, Tall Hat. Think about it," Vitorio ended his rant.

White Bear, a Kiowa war chief who was present, interrupted, "We are here to discuss a plot for assassination, not Apache personal affairs."

"He is right," said Red Cloud, the Lakota. "Tall Hat is trying to wipe our people out of Mother Earth. If we don't seek revenge now, we will regret it forever!" Red Cloud concluded.

"Would everybody please listen? I am Major Broken Arm of the Osage cavalry battalion from Georgia territory. Brigadier General Stand Watie of the First Mounted Rifles Confederacy has sent me for guidance and to change the training location to Cheyenne, Wyoming, to train for this mission."

Geronimo had to speak up. "We shall train right here where we stand!"

"No," replied Major Broken Arm. "Bluecoat is aware of this location, and it is no longer safe here! I brought food rations and water for the trip," Major Broken Arm concluded.

Geronimo was upset, but he wanted to kill Tall Hat so bad that he was willing to sacrifice a comfortable location to get his hands on the evil man killing natives for sport.

"So we will migrate to a different location. But I will bring my chosen warriors."

Major Broken Arm nodded in agreement. They moved on in the meeting, and many warriors spoke.

"Hello, everyone. I am Crazy Horse. This mission is personal to me. It was my brothers that monster killed. I will assist in this mission and kill as many of Tall Hat's men as possible." As Crazy Horse finished speaking, a tear streamed down his cheek. The Apache, the Cherokee, the Kiowa, the Choctaw, the Cree, the Seminole, and the Sioux were all present.

Old Chief Smoke was a Sioux war leader who was Crazy Horse's commander. "I am Chief Smoke. I am Lakota. The white eyes are pouring in from the European nations like ants. All the while, Tall Hat continues to kill our people off. They are colonizing and taking over our land. And like ants, they fight among themselves. They enslaved the Buffalo people and forced them to fight the white eyes war. Even our red brothers and cousins fight alongside graycoat white eyes. We will all die the same death and be buried in the same dirt, but Tall Hat wants to wipe out the red race, and we must stop him for what he has done. So we rest and eat for a few moons, and then we will leave on the trailway that leads to Wyoming. Okay!" said Chief Smoke.

Geronimo said, "Okay, but Lozen will lead the pack. She has the ability to see the enemies before they see us."

Chief Smoke nodded. After the war council meeting, Geronimo lay next to the fire and was fast asleep. He was dreaming a bad dream. He saw his wife running through a burning village, holding their daughter, being shot cowardly in the back by Mexican solider. Then all of a sudden, the scene changed of them all hanging from a tree. It was such a vivid dream, like Geronimo was there. Then he saw a trail of millions of Europeans pouring in. Then he saw his Lakota brothers hanging and burning, and then it was Tall Hat laughing an evil laugh!

THE SKULL THAT YAWNS

Overwhelmed, Geronimo woke suddenly by his nightmare, and he had the sweats. Lozen was already awake.

"Get ready, cousin. We must prepare to go!" Lozen said.

Geronimo nodded in agreement. Then he grabbed a water jug and washed his face with the pouring water. He took a big drink and spit four times in all four directions and said a quick prayer to Ussen for his people and his fallen family for protection here on Earth as well as the afterlife. Geronimo knew that he would see his family again. Wait, something was wrong!

Mangas Coloradas, Geronimo's best friend and warrior, had ran off in the middle of the night. It was the night before anyone saw him ever again. For little did he know, General West would arrest and shoot Mangas for treason as soon as Mangas arrived at his supposed rescue area. Geronimo was mad about Mangas's choice. He had a mission to accomplish. Geronimo grabbed his gear, loaded his horse, and mounted. Lozen was up front with the Lakota, the rest of the tribes and Geronimo in the back. They were all off to Wyoming to practice their big plot to destroy Tall Hat, the most protected man in the world, and to help end this war and genocide.

Geronimo knew that things would never be the same for anybody or tribes in the country. The world would change forever, and the Apache chief knew that his whole life had prepared him for this moment.

CHAPTER 8

Golden Boy Boothe

It was November 4, 1863, and President Abraham Lincoln was in attendance at the Ford Theater. The sixteenth president of the United States would frequent the theater for his relaxation and to spend time with his beloved wife, Mary Todd. The show for the night was the play *Marble Heart*. The main character and starring role in the play was, of course, John Wilkes Booth and the Harry Pearson Grand Combination Company.

Another mysterious character also present the night of was a known Confederate spy, Maria Bell Boyd. The reason for her appearance was to offer Booth a deal that he could not refuse. In fact, no one could or would refuse. A hundred bars of gold. However, he would be the fall guy for a different assassin who would do the actual deed. But Booth would take all the credit for the assassination of the most hated and protected politician in the newfound world.

The Confederacy spies as well as the rest of the public were becoming aware of President Lincoln's visits to the Ford Theater for his own personal entertainment. The first half of the plan was in effect by having the Apache squadron agreeing to the terms of access to Lincoln and "no red man, heroes" policy. The Apache chief did not want credit or fame and fortune for his role in the situation. He just wanted to bring down the king of America.

So the war council plan was for Geronimo to gain access from the back of the building, which was more heavily guarded than the front of the building. Then once inside, he would eliminate the inside guards. No guns were allowed for this stealth mission. It would have to be a subtle knife or bow attack. Then Geronimo and his spirit guide, Lozen, would then get upstairs and eliminate the door guards to gain access to Lincoln's favorite balcony booth. Once they got past the doors, he would eliminate Lincoln fast and retreat hastily back through the window in the bathroom.

John Wilkes Booth would then immediately shoot Lincoln in the face and, by all means necessary, cause a major diversion of attention away from the secret assassins, who would then sneak off the balcony to escape out of the Ford Theater unseen. Once Booth created his diversion of dramatics successfully, Boothe would then escape out the east side of the building, where a horse and buggy would be waiting for Booth.

Ironically, Booth would have done the assassination for free by himself. However, even as famous and well-known as John Booth was, even he had no access to the sixteenth president. Another question at hand for the Confederate war leaders was, would Booth even agree to the terms of this plot? Would John Booth throw away his fame and fortune? John Booth was an established actor in the nation. He had money, wealth, and all of the finer things in life, down to his gold-plated engraved toothbrush! To match his razor, of course.

On top of his wealth, he was easily recognized everywhere he went. He was old money with his family owned cotton stocks, and fortune ran in the family. Young Booth and his brothers all enjoyed luxuries their entire youth. John Booth and his brothers, as adults, enjoyed the benefits of fame, including paid meals and free tailored suits. The Booth boys also had a group of elite Southern-minded friends. The most important friend of Booth would be Edmund Spangler, who happened to be an employee at the Ford Theater.

Spangler, along with the Booth boys, had a Southern cult of personality. So they all had great disdain for Lincoln and any Federal Union minded ideal. People and their different states rights, tariffs, and trades.

The Booth gang attended pubs and social meetings professing their loving Confederate way of life. The gang often joked about kidnapping Honest Abe and holding him for ransom until Abe Lincoln freed all the Confederate prisoners locked up in federal detention centers.

Only problem was, even though John Wilkes Booth had a lot of friends in the militia, John himself was just an actor and a bit lazy. John slept in. He stayed up late gallivanting and partying with his brothers at all the pubs and social elite clubs. John was not known for being rough and rowdy, nor a gunman type. He was more of a fun man. However, he was political and analytical, and he loathed Lincoln and despised him for starting this war for no reason at all other than greed. Booth was seriously annoyed by Lincoln's newfound private security. These assholes would comb the theater and overreact concerning their king's security before every show he attended.

Even though John was already living the perfect life himself, he did not possess the power Lincoln had. John could not understand how a man could start war in every corner of the country. Honest Abe had declared war on the British invaders, the Mormons in Utah, the Apache, and the Lakota Indians. John thought of Lincoln as a power-hungry pig who must be stopped, and here Lincoln was, relaxing and enjoying the theater shows at the Ford Theater.

Lincoln would attend three shows this season. When Lincoln arrived, he would show up with multiple carriages and a large entourage of black uniform soldiers. America was changing now, and now that Abraham had declared the Emancipation Proclamation, he was receiving death threats daily, and his Secret Service men were aware of this fact. Several of John Wilkes Booth's family and friends were Confederate veterans, and some of them were being held at federal prison camps, and this bothered John to know his kin were being detained and that Lincoln was over here enjoying the show.

Maria Belle Boyd was aware of John's imprisoned friend General Lewis, so she knew that John would be a tool in the assassination of Lincoln just off his animosity alone, and with one hundred Confederate gold bars of Confederate-stamped gold stashed away in a barn in Virginia waiting for him to sweeten the deal. After the show and that evening was complete, Bell Boyd stuck around to ask for autographs as a cover-up for her intentions.

After twenty minutes, Belle made her way down a hall that led to the backstage dressing room. When she saw Booth on the sign, she gently knocked and swiftly let herself in through the open door. Immediately, Booth was startled. He was removing his makeup in his mirror and thought she was a groupie going backstage to seduce her favorite actor.

Booth started to raise his voice. "How did you get in here?"

"Mr. Booth, hush down. I'm Belle Boyd. General Powell sent me. Calm down."

"My apologies. I did not recognize your face with that huge hat you have on!" said Booth. "Also, a lot of beautiful young ladies come back to my dressing room for a good time. Is that what you're here for, Ms. Boyd?" Booth finished with a smirk.

"No," rebutted Belle. "I am here on official Confederate business!"

"What business is that now that you have my attention?" John asked.

"Well," started Belle, "I am looking for a man who is willing to shoot that bullshitting federal tyrant in the face. After he is dead, make a grand scene and get paid in gold bars to complete this task."

Booth was bewildered but excited. "I am listening," he said as he continued to remove his makeup.

Our leaders have brainstormed a master plan to breach Abraham's security force and defeat Ambrose goon squad and reach to kill the tyrant. You see, our beloved government has sent dozens of different factions to assassinate that asshole Lincoln, but to no avail. No one came close enough to kill that bastard. We have lost several men and women attempting to defeat Ambrose's stupid security guards, and now we believe we have an outside faction who can accomplish and be successful at terminating Lincoln!"

Booth rebutted, "Well, why would you need me if you already have a source?"

Belle was slightly hesitant to answer. "Well, Mr. Booth, this faction is red man featherheads!"

Booth was a bit confused by the suggestion. "Savage heathens doing White man's work? What in the world is going on? This country is going to hell in a handbasket." He said facetiously

Bell rebutted to his comment, "Mr. Booth, listen. The featherheads have a witch named Lozen. She is psychic, which means she can foresee all the Union soldiers' moves. They can get inside the booth at the Ford Theater, and our leaders refuse to allow the featherheads to take the credit for Lincoln's downfall. The shorty and the witch will stab him strategically to make sure he is leaking out of his neck, and that's where you come in and finish the job and shoot Abe in the face, causing a scene. While the shorty and the witch sneak out of the building unseen, the Confederacy will get all the praise for ending the war and stop the Emancipation Proclamation from spreading to our beloved country. The White man will get accolades. And the best part, Mr. Booth, is that we are guaranteeing your escape and a hundred bars of Confederate-stamped gold!"

Booth was amazed and shocked. A lot went through his mind. He could become the poster boy for the Southern Confederacy. How could those savages really get past Lincoln's security? And was this really happening for him?

"Okay, Belle. My question is, why are these Injuns helping us?"

"It seems as though Grandpa chair-okey actually convinced Jefferson to hire the shorty and his witch sister." she replied. They are all in a rage over the Minnesota hangings. It really ruffled their feathers." Bell laughed. "Geronimo and Sitting Bull had a meeting with our leaders and planned this all out!"

Booth was very excited. "Ms. Belle, just the thought of my family and friends being freed from that horrible prison camp and to be responsible for the fall of the Union government, I will do it! I will go down in history as the Confederate avenger forever! I mean, I would have done it for free, but gold is fun!" Booth joked.

Maria got more serious. "Not a word to a soul about this meeting or the deal is off. Understand?" Belle said as she proceeded to pull a photograph out of her purse and revealed the picture to Booth. It was a picture of the stamped Confederate gold bars stacked in a Garrett barn farms to prove that she was serious. "I will send a messenger soon with further details. Give me about six months," said Belle.

Boothe thought to himself as he stared at the picture, *I will avenge the South.*

As Belle walked out the door, she stopped and nodded. Booth nodded back. Booth was a glory hog and lavished attention. He was gonna do perfect in his role to end the war in the South and free his family and friends from federal prison camps. And free the South.

CHAPTER 9

Doomsday Prepper

The secret new location for training was in Southeast Colorado. Geronimo had been praying and meditating the whole trip from Oklahoma to Colorado trail through Comanche territory. Lozen was able to guide and navigate safely through Colorado. The Cheyenne and Arapaho nations were at war with the Colorado militia, and the Sioux were aware of this conflict. However, Black Kettle and Spotted Owl had already approved of the caravan's safe passage from an earlier meeting.

At a certain point in the trail, Lozen saw warriors strategically placed in the trees along the path, but the Arapaho understood the greater mission at hand with the Apache. The Sioux, along with the graycoats traveling in harmony, were very quietly trotting along. The graycoat soldiers in the caravan were nervous of the Arapaho in the trees. Their hands were on their sidearms, and they were staring at the trees.

Geronimo did not stare. He was lost in his mind for the mission to dethrone Tall Hat.

"Geronimo," Lozen said. "They are letting us pass, but they are uneasy."

So Geronimo raised his voice and said, "Brother, the battle is not with us, and we mean no harm. Just passing through!"

So Geronimo put his hand in the air to show no grabbing weapons. Geronimo was aware that Armageddon and death were all around. Everybody was on edge. However, Geronimo had a deep understanding of the Arapahos stoicism to protect. Besides, Geronimo was already out of his comfort zone by collaborating with other tribes and graycoats. Geronimo knew his mission to kill Tall Hat was far more important than a skirmish with other warriors.

Finally, after twenty more miles north traveling, they arrived at their secret training location. So Geronimo had already contemplated his strategy. Four teams of four to cover all four sides of the Ford Theater building. Also, Geronimo knew who the four teams would consist of. First squad was Eagle Squad—himself, Lozen, Vitorio, Dahteste. The reason being that the Apache knew one another's steps before they were taken. Squad two was Crow Squad, four Sioux—Crazy Horse, Chief Smoke, Red Leaf, and Buffalo Calf Road Woman. Gold Squad were on Osage—Major Broken Arm, General Jubal Early, General Rich Ewell, and Nathan Forest, with three graycoats. Tree Squad would be Black Kettle, Cochise, Black Knife, and Chato.

For the next eight months, all these warriors would train together and synchronize their capabilities. Geronimo was personally given a blueprint layout of the Ford Theater from Major Broken Arm to study and memorize. Geronimo figured a great distraction was needed to kick off the ambush. Geronimo studied the blueprint and saw a path to take to enter after the diversion was created, so he figured to enter a bathroom window that led to the VIP section, up a stairway with a door at the bottom. There would be a guard there for sure. Lincoln had guards everywhere.

Confederate spies already confirmed that Lincoln would attend the Ford Theater frequently with his three hundred henchmen. Lincoln also had a personal bodyguard, Henry Rathbone, who was by his side at all times while they were together in the Ford Theater.

Geronimo was aware of Rathbone's presence. Geronimo wondered what type of warrior Rathbone might be. Oh well, Rathbone would die the same.

Geronimo figured that he would have Team Gold start a fight on the south side of the building and then run off to gain chase. Simultaneously, Team Crow would rain fire on the north side of the building. As Team Crow engaged in a firefight, Team Crow would go to the east side of the building where Team Tree would jump in the fight and avert all attention away from the west side of the building in the back window. That would be reopened by Spangler, Boothe's buddy, and then Eagle Squad would enter the building.

The bathroom window led to the stairs to the VIP entrance. Once inside, all guerilla warfare tactics would be used to eliminate inside guards. Then Geronimo would take it from there. At that point, for Geronimo to execute his revenge on Tall Hat, all he would need to do was eliminate Rathbone. Geronimo would be able to show Tall Hat how he felt about all the atrocities that he committed against the red man.

Now that Geronimo had his plan in place, it was time to train in stealth, speed, and endurance. Geronimo would go over and over the plan for the next eight months. Geronimo knew he would feel when the time was right to attack. After eight months of hiding and training in the Southeast Colorado forest, and it was spring time, perfect for Apache moon, Geronimo felt it was time to execute his plan and justify and redeem his entire race. At all costs. Geronimo knew this was a one-way ticket to glory, but the price of death was worth the price of redemption.

CHAPTER 10

The Human Tiger

It was April 14, 1865. There was a show at the Ford Theater tomorrow. The assassin group had traveled by wagon caravan to Worth, Virginia, where their warhorses were waiting to take the assassins to Washington, DC. While at a pit stop in Virginia, Geronimo and his warriors led a ceremony that night. It was brief.

Geronimo prayed for stealth, protection, and success for this mission. The next day, April 15, 1865, the sun settled in to bring in the quiet evening, and as expected, Honest Abe and his entourage of security arrived at the Ford Theater for the show.

"Our American cousin was the grand show for the evening."

Abraham was in the middle stagecoach of what appeared to be twenty or more stagecoaches. Lincoln was in a good mood that night. He was just recently reelected and had just won the biggest war in modern history. Just five days before show night on April 9, General Robert E. Lee had surrendered at the Appomattox courthouse! However, the plot was already in motion for execution. Lincoln's newfound secret security would surely keep the president and his family safe that evening.

As the show began, the president and his wife, Mary Todd; Lincoln's special guest, Henry Rathbone; and his fiancée went to the balcony VIP seating on the second level. Best view in the house! The show began promptly at 10:15 p.m.

Perfect, Lincoln thought to himself as he put his golden pocket watch away in his coat pocket. Lincoln could sit down and finally enjoy a show in victory.

The Ford Theater had just opened in early 1863, so other times, when Lincoln attended the show with his wife, he was in wartime. *Finally, some peace,* Lincoln thought as he looked all around the stage while the show was going on. At 10:35 p.m., just twenty minutes into the show, suddenly, the secret security on the southside of the building were ambushed. Arrows flew from all directions. Then the opposite side of the building was attacked simultaneously, and chaos ensued outside the theater. Twenty guards were instantly killed. The security was so confused they halted their own gunfire to rush where they thought the arrows were flying from. The guards ran in circles while a second barrage of arrows rained down on the security guards.

All of a sudden, arrows stopped flying, and eight horsemen trotted off in the east direction and stamped off like lightning. At least forty guards gave chase. Another hail of arrows flew in from the north side of the building. Not all secret security had rifles or pistols. Only half were gunners and snipers. The other half were engineers and hand combat specialist. Gunfire erupted on the building's west side. However, because of a victory parade the day before, people were celebrating with fireworks, booze, and gunshots, so loud bangs were not unusual in Washington, DC. Now with chaos completely taking over, Eagle Squad entered through the west side back window that was left open by Ed Spangler, Boothe's buddy. Vitorio decided that he and Dahteste would stand guard at the window while Lozen and Geronimo proceeded. Vitorio figured if an urgent escape was needed, he, Dahteste, could assist better from that window.

All of a sudden, a guard running back to his post ran toward Geronimo and Lozen. However, Geronimo threw a knife directly at the guard's throat, killing him instantly. Geronimo then began creeping up the staircase that connected a downstairs bathroom to the upstairs dressing room that led to the VIP balcony. Once they were upstairs, there were two sleeping guards securing the VIP balcony room. As Lozen and Geronimo crouched in darkness at the top of the staircase, Lozen pulled out her medicine bag and opened it to reveal a glass marble she found years back following a wagon train of German settlers. As soon as the marble slowly rolled toward the sleeping guards, one awoke and bent over to pick the marble up. An arrow immediately flew over his head, striking his dead sleeping partner behind him. As soon as he looked up, a flying knife struck him in the throat, killing him instantly.

Lozen then stood by the closed door and waved her hands over the door with closed eyes to implement her spiritual infrared. Lozen threw open her eyes and gave Geronimo sign language of two and two. Two women, two men. Geronimo nodded that he understood what she was saying. Geronimo then took a deep breath while rubbing the medicine bag he wore around his neck. And at this moment, he knew.

Geronimo quickly opened the door to rush Lincoln, but Rathbone jumped in front of the president. Geronimo's arm was just long enough to swing a haymaker and stab Lincoln in his jugular before Rathbone could shield him. As Rathbone and his fiancée realized that they were being attacked, Lozen came in from behind and clubbed Rathbone's fiancée, Clara Harris, in the head unconscious. Rathbone then tackled Geronimo, and as they were scuffling, Geronimo sliced Rathbone's arm, trying to stab him in the throat, but Rathbone blocked the deadly blow with his shoulder.

In the meantime, Mary was petrified with fear at what she was witnessing. Once Geronimo damaged Rathbone enough with punches to his face, Geronimo then took his buckhorn knife out of Rathbone's shoulder and then immediately stuck the knife in Tall Hat's left thigh. Lincoln looked Geronimo in the eye as he was frozen in fear. He was holding his throat while blood gushed from his throat. As Lincoln looked down at the knife, Geronimo thought to himself, *This is my grandfather's knife.*

Geronimo wiped the bloody knife on Lincoln's jacket, leaned over, and whispered, "We're even."

Immediately, John Wilkes Booth jumped from behind and pushed Geronimo down and screamed, "Sic Semper Tyrannis!"

Everyone in the crowd looked up and only saw Booth standing there while Geronimo and Lozen crawled out and down the staircase and back out the window. They disappeared as if they were ghosts.

Back in the theater, Booth screamed, "Kill the tyrant!" as he jumped and tripped over Rathbone, who was knocked out on the floor. As he tripped, he pulled his derringer gun and aimed for Lincoln's face but missed and hit him on the back of the head.

Booth panicked, and instead of running back the same door, being loyal to his diversion, he jumped on the curtain and swung, landing on the stage as the curtain ripped down. Booth broke his leg as he fell. Booth, determined to escape, limped offstage out the back where a horse and buggy was waiting for him. It was part of the arrangement.

John's leg was hurt, but his excitement caused him to laugh as he was carted off to Garrett Farms to retrieve his gold bars then to Port Royal, Virginia, to retrieve his case and escape to Europe to live the rest of his life.

"Garrett Farms, here I come. Yeehaw!" he yelled out, in excitement.

Booth would be on the run for twelve days once the Federal Union Army were aware of his whereabouts. JR West platoon surrounded the haybarn building where Booth was hiding with his gold, but he didn't know who to trust to help him ship his gold, so he was stuck.

General JR West shouted, "Come out with your hands up, John! Now!"

As soon as verbal response was heard from Booth, the army opened fire on the barn, turning the barn into Swiss cheese. General West entered the building with rifle mounted to his shoulder to discover Booth shot multiple times and bleeding profusely. He was lying on top of a pile of gold bars.

Dripping blood filled the engraved CSA letters, drowning the gold as the letters disappeared in a sea of blood. All the Booth brothers and Edmund Spangler were hung to death by rope for treason. And the internal investigations sector of the new USA launched a major investigation, questioning Rathbone, Mary Todd, and Clara Harris, the only three witnesses inside the VIP balcony that night.

THE SKULL THAT YAWNS

Mary Todd was called first to the federal headquarters building. She noticed that Henry Rathbone was already there. Mary Todd was traumatized and highly upset, and she did not want to talk with Henry or anyone for that matter. However, General Ulysses S. Grant escorted his family friend and recently widowed Mary Todd to the questioning room.

"Please have a seat, Mary," Grant said.

Mary sat down nervously, twiddling her thumbs while she looked down. Another detective entered the room to help with questioning and put the pieces to the puzzle together to figure out how the Secret Service was breached and their commander in chief executed so hatefully.

Mary had a blank look in her face. She was pale and emaciated for she had not slept or ate since the incident. Mary had just witnessed the violent death of her beloved husband. She was a bundle of nerves. The detective opened his mouth. Mary started screaming in a nervous breakdown.

"It was a red man heathen savage demon who murdered my sweet Abraham!" she burst into emotional rage.

She wiped the papers off the desk and threw books. General Grant tried to calm her down, but she was too upset.

"That damn savage breed!" she yelled as she picked up her chair and attempted to throw it through the window. The detective grabbed the chair and set it down. Mary fell to the ground, punching the floor.

She continued her rant as she rolled on the ground. "It was a red man Injun who entered the balcony first and stabbed Abraham first. Booth shot Abraham after he got stabbed in the neck by that demon heathen."

The detective had Mary detained and ordered the local mental institution for further observation, and the situation was no better for Henry Rathbone or Clara Harris. They all had the same story! A red man savage somehow got past world-class security and broke into the protected Ford Theater and assassinated the most famous man in the world.

Impossible, General Grant thought. *There is no way that a savage could pull off such an elite, complex task. Not even possible.*

Henry Rathbone and Clara Harris were also admitted to the mental institution for further observation. The general and detective did not believe the savage story. Clara Harris committed suicide while in custody, so other than Mary Todd and Henry Rathbone, no one saw this red man. No one.

ABOUT THE AUTHOR

Anthony was born in Oakland, California, raised in Bangor, California. He now resides in Oroville, California. To everyone who believed in him, thank you for reading *The Skull That Yawns*!

Printed in the USA
CPSIA information can be obtained
at www.ICGtesting.com
LVHW091504051124
795745LV00001B/187